How I Learned to Swim

Somebody Jones

T0357534

methuen | drama

LONDON · NEW YORK · OXFORD · NEW DELHI · SYDNEY

METHUEN DRAMA
Bloomsbury Publishing Plc
50 Bedford Square, London, WC1B 3DP, UK
1385 Broadway, New York, NY 10018, USA
29 Earlsfort Terrace, Dublin 2, Ireland

BLOOMSBURY, METHUEN DRAMA and the Methuen
Drama logo are trademarks of Bloomsbury Publishing Plc

First published in Great Britain by Methuen Drama in 2024

Cover design by Eleanor Rose

Cover photo by Bradley Martin

A catalogue record for this book is available from the British Library.

A catalog record for this book is available from the Library of Congress.

ISBN: PB: 978-1-3505-2449-1
ePDF: 978-1-3505-2450-7
eBook: 978-1-3505-2451-4

Series: Modern Plays

Typeset by Mark Heslington Ltd, Scarborough, North Yorkshire
Printed and bound in Great Britain

To find out more about our authors and books visit
www.bloomsbury.com and sign up for our newsletters.

HOW I LEARNED TO SWIM

by Somebody Jones

CAST

JAMIE   Frankie Hart

CREATIVES

Director/Dramaturg   Emma Jude Harris

Designer   Debbie Duru

Lighting Designer   Ali Hunter

Sound Designer/Composer   Nicola T. Chang

Associate Sound Designer   Hattie North

Producer   Rebecca Prentice

Technical Stage Manager   Josephine Shipp

Assistant Stage Manager   Leigh Arthur

The tour was kindly supported by Arts Council England and the Keep it Fringe Fund.

HOW I LEARNED TO SWIM was first performed at Paines Plough's Roundabout at Edinburgh Festival Fringe on 2 August 2024, then transferred to Brixton House and Bristol Old Vic in September.

Produced by Prentice Productions

Prentice Productions is a UK-based theatre and film production company with a focus on new writing, queer and female-led narratives. We prioritise work that is imaginative, political and which centres diverse experiences. We champion artists who are creating exceptional work with little resources and want to make work that is impossible to ignore.

Recent theatre productions include: *Jobsworth* (Pleasance Theatre and New Diorama Theatre), *30 and Out* (Soho Theatre, Pleasance Edinburgh, 53Two, The Actors, Omnibus Theatre, Pleasance Islington), *Mermaid* (Theatre503), *Gigi Star* (Applecart Arts). *30 and Out* by Kit Sinclair is currently being developed for TV.

For screen, Prentice Productions presented *The Pirate* which screened internationally at film festivals, winning four awards including "Best Story". Two shorts are entering the festival circuit in 2024, *Driving with Tim* starring Simon Callow and *House Hunters*, in post-production with Molinare. We have two shorts in pre-production and three shorts in development with exciting new writers.

In Association with Brixton House

Brixton House is a modern arts venue in South London. An inspired vision to build a cultural hub centred on the legacy of the former Ovalhouse. The new multi-arts venue, with a particular focus on theatre, tells stories from undervalued, unheard voices and excluded communities that represent its home in the heart of Brixton. Its arts programme reflects the rich and authentic storytelling of local and international diverse communities and champions innovative and creative entrepreneurial perspectives.

A place for people to come together to create and enjoy performance, the venue houses two theatres and performance spaces, seven rehearsal rooms, meeting rooms, office space dedicated to creative organisations as well as a public cafe and bar. Brixton House is generously supported by London Borough of Lambeth, Arts Council England, Garfield Weston Foundation, The Wolfson Foundation, Cockayne Grants for the Arts, London Community Fund, The 29th May 1961 Charitable Trust.

Director's note

by Emma Jude Harris

In the making of this show I have sometimes been struck by the fact that Somebody and I both grew up in Los Angeles, with our paths never crossing until we finally connected on X (formerly Twitter, RIP). This only happened after we had each relocated all the way across the Atlantic Ocean, in our respective emigration journeys to London as graduate students and lovers of live theater (as opposed to TV/film, that glossy chimera lusted over in California).

Throughout my research process, one of my touchstones has been a 2008 exhibition at the UCLA Fowler Museum entitled *Mami Wata: Arts for Water Spirits in Africa and Its Diasporas* (guest-curated by Henry John Drewal). Through that exhibition, I encountered the work of multimedia artists Eve Sandler and Sonya Clark, which has informed many fruitful conversations between myself and designer Debbie Duru. Reading about the exhibition also led us to visual artists Howardena Pindell and María Magdalena Campos-Pons, as well as scuba diver/photographer Ayana V Jackson, whose recent series *From the Deep: In the Wake of Drexciya* resonates profoundly with *Swim*'s themes.

In 2008, Somebody and I were both attending high school in Los Angeles. The entire time the exhibition was open (April–August 2008), I was probably, on average, fewer than five miles away. Fourteen years later, now that Somebody and I both reside in

London, 5500 miles from Los Angeles, it seems wild to think there was a point in space and time when I was only a thirty-minute walk from the research I would find myself needing to do more than a decade later. As I scoured Google Images and YouTube trying in vain to find the exhibition catalog, I have occasionally kicked my teenage self for not having had the foresight to attend that exhibition.

However, as the character Jamie learns, time is not a straight line.

How I Learned to Swim reverberates across many planes and genres, including magic realism, mythopoetry, memorial, diasporic ritual, and coming-of-age story. It's about grappling with personal and ancestral grief; Black diasporic belonging in the United States; and recontextualizing one's traumatic relationship to the elements; it is, of course, also about learning to swim, not to mention unlearning (and unloading) baggage. Whew! There is *so* much to explore!

It is a privilege to direct and dramaturg *How I Learned to Swim.* I'm so grateful to be working with such a wonderful team on this athletic and expansive piece about acceptance, resilience, and life after loss.

THANK YOU
by Somebody Jones

Jack, my partner in life/crime (husband), for reading every single draft, being at every show, and generally just being my biggest hype man.

Dad, Grandmommy, and Auntie—thank you for coming to every show and for always being my biggest cheerleaders. Special thanks to Dad for flying all the way to London for my first ever production.

To my late cat, Chewy—you didn't make it to see this draft, but you were always on my lap (or screaming) for the others. You will forever be the best writing partner.

My besties: Abbie Grundy, Aizehi Nomo, Alec Engerson, and Jedidah Fernandez-DoQui—y'all are my rock! Thanks for supporting from across the pond (yes, you too Abbie because South London does feel that far away).

Khadifa Wong—I will never forget how we only had three weeks before the Footprints Festival deadline, and you told me that of course I could write a whole play in that time that only had one or two actors, no set, and minimal costumes/props/lights/sound. You believed in me when I didn't, and now I've got this gorgeous play because of it.

Thank you to Jermyn Street Theatre for giving the work-in-progress version of this play a platform during Footprints and special thanks to Penny

Horner, Jessie Mckenzie, and Merryl Ansah. Merryl—thank you for being the first person to read for Jamie and for this stunning cover.

To my always positive and reassuring agent, Kara Fitzpatrick—thank you for choosing to represent me and for going on this journey with me. You've been such an encouraging voice through all of the highs and lows of this play.

Thank you to the entire Paines Plough team for programming my first play and for letting me bother you all every Wednesday for seven months—Debo Adebayo, Charlotte Bennett, Jodie Gilliam, Manwah Siu, Ellie Fitz-Gerald, and Mrin Roy. A special thank you to Katie Posner for telling me in 2023 when we ran into each other at a press night that you never stopped thinking about this play, kicking off our Roundabout conversation.

Ben Quashie and the Brixton House team, and Nancy Medina and the Bristol Old Vic team. Nancy—thank you also for inspiring the addition of Lasirèn.

To Anthony Simpson-Pike—thank you for reading this play and telling me about Drexciya. This play is even more mythical because of you.

To the fabulous Commissioning Editor at Methuen Drama, Callan McCarthy, and the Methuen Drama team for publishing my first play and for this gorgeous playtext. Eleanor Rose—you did a stellar job; and Bradley Martin—what a striking photo.

Thank you to early supporters of this play: Jaquita Ta'le, Dr Fiona Graham, Daniel Bailey, Simon Jaggers, the Women's Prize for Playwriting team, Jessica Kubzansky, Emilie Beck, and the Boston Court Playhouse team.

A big SHOUT OUT to my creative team—Frankie Hart, Debbie Duru, Nicola T. Change, Ali Hunter, Josephine Shipp, Hattie North, and Leigh Arthur. We've truly made magic together and I can't thank you all enough for all of your ideas, kindness, and just generally being the best at what you all do.

Rebecca Prentice—this production would not have happened if it wasn't for you answering my Twitter callout back in early 2023. And we have been through it! Thank you for sticking with me through all of the no's and almost yes's with this play. You've been such an incredible producer and friend.

To Emma Jude Harris—I couldn't have asked for a better director or dramaturg. I loved every single dramaturgy session and getting to geek out about research with you. Your passion and dedication to this play has really carried me through some tough moments this year. This play is so much more eerie, enchanting, and overall strong because of you.

How I Learned to Swim

Somebody Jones

Characters

Jamie (she/her)—Black and/or mixed, thirty years old.

Time

Now.

Setting

I imagine that Jamie and Bas's parents live in View Park, Bas likes to surf in Malibu, Babalawo's office is in Koreatown, and Jamie probably goes to the Y in Hollywood.

I'm a proud Californian, so California is soaked into this play (can't get enough water puns), but how important is this to the play?

Only a drop.

The play could be set in any coastal state in the U.S.

What is important, though, is that we go on this journey together. So grab my hand, the water's warm. Trust me. Let's jump on 1?

3

2

Scene One

A family pool. Kids' screams. A very overstimulated family pet. There's probably a soggy hotdog on the ground too, because there always is at these things.

Jamie *sits poolside. A memory has her in a chokehold.*

Jamie   Legslegslegslegs armsarms, legslegslegslegs armsarms . . .

My first pool party. Katie Jørgensen's ninth birthday.

"The water won't bite."

As if that helped. I kept wondering why our mom brought us to a pool party when she knew we couldn't swim. Well, that I couldn't swim.

"You don't have to worry about your hair, I'll do it tomorrow."

I had just hit the age when you start realizing that you can't use any of the hair products in your friend's bathrooms if they have names like Katie Jørgensen. Definitely safe with Dami Adebayo and Kaya Makeba, and maybe Mia Jackson if you're willing to take a chance on Just for Me. Her bathroom cabinet was a real gamble. And I'm not the betting type.

"I'm just going to watch."

"Well at least put your feet in."

Maybe Dad was embarrassed that I couldn't swim. Didn't want to live up to the stereotype. But it was fine either way because Bas made up for it.

"CANNONBALL!"

That's my little brother, always the first one in. I think the only reason why our parents got us swim lessons was because Bas kept jumping in. The ocean, a pool, the sewer — that's where they drew the line. If he was going to keep trying to become a fish, at least he wouldn't get hurt in the process. So you can only imagine how guilty they feel now.

Legslegslegslegs armsarms, legslegslegslegs armsarms . . .

Brianna and James are always trying to outdo each other. Today it's laps in the pool. Next week it'll be our big math test. One day it could even be blowjobs. Their codependence is laughable now, but it won't be when James dies in a freak accident where a tree lands on his car, and Brianna replaces the blood in her veins with heroin. But like I said, today, it's just laps in the pool.

Which is fine for me because if they're doing laps, that means there's no room for me to swim. Bas's cannonballs made them restart their competition, so they've pushed everyone to the shallow end. And with a game of chicken monopolizing the pool, I barely have enough room to put my feet in.

"You getting in JAYYYYYY-MIIIIIII?"

I hate the way Kyle says my name. He says it like he's on the Gravitron at the Easter Fair.

Like my name is going back in time in his mouth, collecting sounds on the way.

"You're too scared to get your precious hair wet huh?"

As if he'd know anything about hair. Honestly looks like he brushes his hair with a rake.

"It's too cold."

I don't know why I gave him an excuse. I know better than to talk to the class bully. When you take the bait, they've got you. Only reason why the Jørgensen parents made Katie invite him is cuz his parents are Danish immigrants too. Gotta stick together and shit I guess.

"Here, I'll help you get used to it!"

It's annoying when he starts splashing me, but it quickly turns terrifying when he starts dragging me.

In a party of nine-year-olds, screams aren't a sign of danger. Screams mean that everything is going great. Better than great. It's the silence you have to worry about.

It doesn't matter anyway because you can't scream for long if your head is under water.

"Yuuurb drowwwwwning meeeeh . . ."

He can't hear me though. And even if he did, would he care? So I fight for my life. I punch and I kick and I punch and I kick, and finally, I make contact.

Kyle didn't even make it past the shallow end. There was so much blood.

The   silence   is what alerted the parents that something was wrong. Then the wave of screams hit like a tsunami. You would have really believed that sharks lived in the deep end. You ever dropped paint into water? That's what the pool looked like. Swirls of red mixing with blue.

That day taught me to always go for the nose.

Kyle's parents weren't as mad as I thought they should be. Maybe cuz I was a girl? Sexist. Or maybe it was because this wasn't new for Kyle.

"He's been having a tough time since we moved from Copenhagen."

My parents didn't care about the "tough time" he'd been having and wanted him suspended anyway. But since this didn't happen on school grounds, there was nothing they could really do.

There was no more legslegslegslegs armsarms, legslegslegslegs armsarms after that. I never went to another pool party. And that was just the beginning of water taking things away from me.

Scene Two

A pool with too much chlorine. But better safe than sorry at the YMCA.

Jamie   I'm thirty years old and I'm going to take my first swim lesson.

I say it like a mantra in my car mirror before walking into the Y.

I'm thirty years old and I'm going to take my FIRST swim lesson. I'm thirty years old and I'm GOING to take my first swim lesson.

Even though the pools are in the back, the second I walk in, I smell anxiety. Or chlorine. I think they both smell the same.

I go to tap in and I know her. The instructor at the desk. I know her name before she says it.

"Molly."

I almost want to tell her that I know who she is, but would that be creepy? I think that would be creepy.

"Jamie."

"Welcome Jamie! If you need anything, let me know. Cheers!"

Her British accent would almost be comical if it wasn't real.

Molly Scofield. Her Y profile read: "Turned thirty this year" (like me). "Working on my master's" (like me again). "Favorite ice cream is Rocky Road" (so similar it's scary). "I can teach anyone to swim."

I hope I'm not the exception.

Basketball courts, the locker room, a dance studio. And then I find myself leaning over the pool. Staring into the artificial blue water.

I hear the plop plopping sound of kids jumping feet knees head first into water. Plop plop.

What don't I like about water? Don't get me started.

First of all it's wet. Second of all it probably always wants to kill you. Third of all it's wet. I'm thirty years old and I'm GOING to take my first swim lesson. I don't think this is working.

My reflection in the water looks like a fun house mirror. Cheeks into nose, nose into chin. I feel like I'm f a d i n g.

PLOP.

I'm immediately submerged in water. There's gushing swishing swirling sounds and wobbly figures above me. I am IN the fun house mirror. I gasp for air as I reach for the edge of the pool. Thank God it was only the four-feet section.

"I got her!"

Little wet feet scurry away with laughter trailing behind them.

"Did you see her face when you pushed her?"

A dance studio, the locker room, basketball courts.

I'm thirty years old and I'm NOT going to take my first swim lesson. I say it like a mantra in my car mirror before driving home.

Scene Three

That dreaded pool.

Jamie   "Does this pool have that pee dye stuff?"

"Does it have what?!"

You know when you know someone knows what you're talking about, but they pretend not to know? You know?

I got pressured to come back by an email. An automated "we missed you!" guilt trip. Well . . . that and Bas. My phone reminded me that his birthday is in two weeks.

"It's just that I'm on my period."

Oh my God I'm so awkward. But Molly is nice about it. If she remembers me from yesterday, she doesn't show it.

"You'll be fine. That stuff is a myth anyway. The guy who 'made' it in like the fifties or whatever was just playing a prank."

"Eh, I don't know."

"Plus, if you're on your period, you should be more worried about sharks."

"What!"

"Jokes. The Y released all of the sharks this morning. Why don't you tell me why you're here?"

This is a hard question. Both the long and the short answer sound a little ridiculous, especially to a stranger. So I opt for:

"I just want to be more confident in the water."

Which is not a total lie.

"Let's get in then!"

I like how she says "let's" like she's not already waist deep in the water and I'm not standing outside of the pool, looking down at her.

I tell Molly that swimming is colonialist and she laughs in my face.

"I've never heard that one before."

But it's true. There's a reason why we haven't explored the deepest parts of the ocean. She doesn't want us to colonize her. But Mars doesn't care. The minute we can sustain life there, it'll be a war. Mars, the new Africa. Call it the Mars Berlin Conference.

"I think I can change your mind about water."

"Molly, we just met and you're already setting yourself up for failure."

"Ha! Can I tell you why I became a swim instructor?"

"Go for it."

"Paul Marshall and Kevin Burns."

These are two names that I've definitely never heard of. David Isom is the name I know. A skinny nineteen-year-old who thought he deserved to swim just as much as the white man. But 1950s Florida wasn't ready for him. After David swam in a formerly segregated public pool, it would be a whole year before another Black person was allowed in. And all this was happening in the States, while Marshall and Burns hadn't even been born yet.

"People actually thought that Black people were too heavy to swim."

Now it's my turn to laugh. I'm the first to say that Americans believe in some wild things, but this is rich.

"I know. I know."

"I thought Americans were ridiculous."

"Who do you think taught you how to be ridiculous?"

She's got a point there.

"Black Brits literally thought, and some still do think, that we naturally sink in water. That our bones are too dense. But with Paul Marshall and Kevin Burns being the first Black swimmers to represent Britain in the Olympics, I think they changed a few minds. They changed mine."

Then she tells me about feeling like the only one, and I know that feeling all too well. The only one who had to protect her hair. The only one who looked like her in the pool. But no matter what, she was going to do what she loved, even if she was the only one.

"You ready?"

And just like that, I completely forgot that I came here for swim lessons.

"I don't know. The last time someone forced a Black person into water, that didn't end well for us. 400 years later and we're still dealing with it."

Eeep!

The splash of water on my shins is cold, but surprisingly more refreshing than uncomfortable.

"You gotta get in the water to get me back!"

Again, she does have a point.

"Fine, but just a toe."

"See. Progress. We're getting somewhere now."

"Don't get too excited."

But one toe turns into two toes into three into ankle knee hip and here I am. Jamie is actually in a pool.

The water is warm. Maybe too warm. My mind flashes back to the pee dye. I'm not even on my period.

"You did it!"

Is my new car ride home mantra.

Scene Four

Stiff seats. New car smell. Even the conversation feels leathery.

Jamie   I didn't tell Mom that I'd done my first swim lesson. She doesn't even know I'm taking them. There will just be too many questions, like she's asking right now.

"Are you excited?"

She's been buying a lot of new things lately. Like this car. And getting a lot of new hobbies. Knitting turned into cryptocurrency turned into seeking a spiritual guide. Dad says it's grief. I'm for sure not grieving, so I'm not sure why Mom is. It's not like Bas is dead. He's just missing. There's a difference.

"Just let your mom have this."

Ok fine! But I'm not going to like it!

"Met anyone lately?"

Here come the questions.

"Not that you have to! I'm just asking. Have you been getting out more? Exercising at all? Got any trips planned? I was thinking we should have a little girls trip. Just us. Would you like that? — Oh, is this it?"

Both of us are unsure where we are going. Physically and spiritually.

Parked in front of what looks like a collection of abandoned office buildings, I'm sure we're at the wrong place. But nope! This is it. You'd think a "father of mysteries" would have a fancier place.

Babalawo, that's what he tells us to call him. Fine. Cool. Whatever.

"Do you know of Mami Wata?"

There are obviously two answers to this. One will end this session right here and now, which is what I want, but the other—

"No! Who is that?"

Bas obviously got his wild curiosity from Mom. And I got my steadfast logic from Dad. And so it begins.

Babalawo tells us a story about the water god, Mami Wata.

One day, a poor fisherman goes out to sea to make money for his family. But the waves are violent that day. A storm no doubt is on the horizon, which of course isn't good for the fisherman, because rough waters mean no money and no money means no food. And he just learned that his wife is pregnant. Again. So he tries. But the fish know just as well as he does.

After hours on the water, he decides to go home. Slowly pulling his boat back to shore, he wrestles with himself about what to do and what to say to his wife and two children. And then he sees it. A gold mirror! They would never go hungry again.

But this fisherman is no thief. He looks around for the owner, but there's not a soul in sight. So he takes it, wraps it in his shirt, and heads home with a newfound energy.

When his wife sees him, she kisses him. It's a kiss that feels like hope. They sleep intertwined that night, with the fisherman's hand on his wife's belly. But he doesn't sleep well.

Someone visits him in his dream. A woman with scaly skin and long black hair. She tells him that he must return the mirror or he'll be cursed forever. "You don't believe in me?" she snorts. The fisherman can't help but laugh. "Spirits aren't real," he thinks, "only starvation."

"Whatever you decide," she says, "you won't have to worry about your family anymore."

In the morning, he tells his wife to sell the mirror for as much as she can get. She returns that evening with enough money to buy them food for the rest of the year and then some. They decide to celebrate that night with a feast. So the fisherman goes to fetch his son and daughter from the beach, to tell them of the good news. But with each step closer to the water, the storm from yesterday roars louder. Unable to hear his own voice, the fisherman finds himself screaming for his children.

When he reaches the water, he sees a woman. Instinctively, he grabs her arm to pull her closer to safety. But when she turns around, the fisherman screams. Her skin as glowing as emeralds, her eyes like those of a fish, her mouth a tangled weave of seaweed and shark's teeth. "You can only save one" she says, and dives into the water. Her dolphin fin flapping behind her.

Then, he sees them—his two children screaming and waving in the ocean. Now he understands. He swims towards them with all of his might, but they're too far apart. He'll never reach both of them in time! "Swim to me!" he cries, but he can't see the seaweed ropes wrapped around their legs, tying them in place.

So, he makes his choice.

With his son being the stronger swimmer, he goes to his daughter first, hoping that his son will swim to safety.

After grabbing his daughter, he turns to find his son. But he's gone. Mami Wata laughs and her cackles turn into thunder.

That night, Mami Wata stole three things from the fisherman—his newfound riches, his hope, and his son.

Babalawo says he thinks we're cursed.

"That'll be $52.50."

"What's the extra $2.50 for?"

"5% mandatory service charge."

Scene Five

Another day, another lesson.

Jamie   Lesson 2 of Molly's School of Swim is to get used to not breathing under water. Which is literally dying.

"No, you're not dying. You don't hold your breath. Just blow bubbles."

"Blow bubbles?"

"It's fun."

It is in fact not fun, but Molly explains that it's actually an important part of swimming. You need to get used to exhaling when your face is in water so that when you come up for air, you automatically inhale.

"Am I supposed to be having fun now?"

Molly laughs. But blowing bubbles and coming up for air is harder than it sounds. I end up just holding my breath most of the time. Which, when your face is submerged in water, feels exactly like dying. After a couple reps of this, all I see is red, so we move on to floating, which somehow feels worse.

"Jussss relashhhhhh."

"What?"

It's like when a dentist starts asking you about your day while they're pillaging through your mouth treasures.

"Just relax."

Apparently floating is actually one of the more difficult things for new swimmers to grasp. It's not because it's physically hard, you basically don't do anything, but because you have no support.

"Tilt your head back. Chin to the sky. I know it sounds weird, but it works."

And she's not wrong. Maybe it's the fact that my brain is too focused on pointing my chin up to be anxious, but whatever it is, it's working.

"Don't worry. I got you."

I'm weightless in her hands. If this is what swimming is about, I could do this all day. My heartbeat starts matching the slow swish of the pool. We're the only two people here. This feels like a feeling worth chasing. Is this why you like water so much, Bas?

But then I'm

s
    i
       n
         k
          i
           n
            g.

Stiff panic shoots through my body and I'm watching my world blur like this isn't my favorite place to be. It's peaceful in a depressing sort of way.

"Jamie!"

Molly pulls me out of the water's clutches.

"I didn't think you would sink!"

"Well, that makes two of us!"

I take swallows of air.

"Let's take a break."

"Good idea . . . I'll never find him."

"What?"

Fuck. I meant to say that in my head.

"Nothing."

She creases her nose. She knows I'm lying, but she doesn't ask. I don't tell. And we just sit there.

Our silence is so loud that you can hear the tick ticking of the giant clock on the wall.

"Wanna practice kicking your feet?"

"No."

"Maybe some arm movements?"

"I think I might be done for today."

"You'll always be safe in the water. You belong here, Jamie."

"What?"

Molly motions for me to sit next to her. It's story time, I can feel it.

"You ever heard of Drexciya?"

I tell Molly that opioids aren't my thing and she laughs. Then she tells me about "Black Atlantis," Drexciya. The myth goes that pregnant Africans who jumped from slave ships gave birth to babies with gills. These babies created Drexciya—an underwater utopia for the almost enslaved.

"When land no longer seemed like a hospitable place for them, our ancestors created a new world. So the water is nothing to be afraid of. I know you feel a pull when you're in water. I feel it too. We belong here."

"If you just made that up, Molly, to get me back in the water, I'm not gunna do it, but I gotta commend you for effort."

Molly just smiles and says, "See you next week, then?"

And like that, the lesson is over.

Scene Six

The past. A competition. Little white boats dot a too blue ocean. Someone's making a joke to lighten the mood. The kind of day that feels like it's full of possibilities.

Jamie   I had always been skeptical before, obviously, but I think I really stopped trusting water when I saw it almost kill someone.

Bas and I had always begged Mom to take us to Haiti. The second she told us we were part Haitian, we were determined to go. But she always had an excuse. So once we got old enough to travel, we grabbed some friends and went on our own.

Mia and I thought this was just going to be a chill beach vacation. Bathing suits, tan, palm trees, sun, cocktails, food, massages, aaaaahhhhhhhh. But Bas and Llanzo had other plans.

I had never even heard of a freediving competition before. After the event, Mia made a point to walk around puddles. The curtains stayed closed in our ocean-view room.

"We shouldn't have come here."

She wouldn't even drink water. We had to beg her to drink juice.

"This is why Black people don't belong in the ocean."

Sosa was the only one who looked like us in the competition. Yeah, she didn't speak English, but to Mia, she was still one of us.

Mia moved back home when we were kids, and grew up in a state that automatically became California when anyone asked. Because even Americans can barely place Ohio on a map. And she wasn't from beach Cleveland, or brewery Cleveland, but Black Cleveland. Where swim lessons cost money and do you have water money? I didn't think so. Life was more about trying to figure out how you were going to afford college than worrying about the water. Praying every night that Ohio god-fairy LeBron would grant you a scholarship. What did the ocean have to do with that?

"This is so cool!"

Bas was enchanted, as always, by anything water related. This was his idea of course. And his buddy Llanzo just ate it up.

Llanzo, Jamaican born, Queens raised. So he had a different relationship to water. Every summer, from 9AM to 5PM, he spent his days with his siblings, between two pools and six miles of sand and ocean. The beach was his babysitter.

"Pops would just leave us there and go to work. It's a surprise none of us ever got hurt. The nineties were a wild time."

Wild indeed. But not as wild as this.

The judges explained the rules: Declare, retrieve, protocol, score. Declare how far you intend to dive, retrieve the flag at your declared depth, follow protocol when you surface, then wait for your score. It all sounds pretty easy until you see it.

Sosa was up first. She held onto the rope before her dive. It would be the only thing guiding her in the darkness. She flashed us a smile before going under. I see that smile in my nightmares.

Sosa declared 203 feet. About the size of a fourteen-story building and more than the national female record at the time. If the judges were surprised, they didn't show it. I think even Bas whispered a wow.

With a quiet splash, Sosa went under, and so did the medics. In case. In case what? This was the open ocean and she didn't have any gear. Anything could happen.

"She's been gone for a while."

If Llanzo was worried, I was worried. And that was only at the one-minute mark. At two minutes, Bas had something to say. His bouncy energy kept making me nervous. Every time he saw a bubble, I could feel him pointing. As if to say, "there she is!"

Not long after, Mia was wondering if she was ever going to come back.

When a diver surfaces, they're supposed to take a few clean breaths above water, then give a hand signal that they're ok.

When Sosa emerged, she immediately passed out. Blood flowed from her nose. I got flashbacks of Kyle.

The medic was tapping her cheeks, saying Sosa

SOSA SOSA!

They rushed us away after that. If this was going to be her last moments, they wanted to give her some privacy. That and not having any witnesses for this PR nightmare.

We didn't say much after the competition. And none of us dared to look up Sosa's name. In the end, she had gone without oxygen for three minutes. She was probably dead, and none of us wanted confirmation. Call her Schrödinger's Sosa.

We certainly didn't go to the beach again after that. But Bas was back at it the next day. He said the water was calling him. I always wonder about that. How that moment didn't faze him.

Mia was finally drinking juice by then. Llanzo started closing the curtains too. He'd be back in the water in a couple months, but this vacation definitely changed him. Now he knew what the water was capable of.

Welcome to the club, buddy.

Scene Seven

The big lesson.

Jamie   Molly has lost her mind. The deep end??? I can barely get a hold of the shallow end, let alone the DEEP END.

"Trust me."

I don't wanna. But she says I'm ready. We've practiced everything. Even legslegslegslegs armsarms, legslegslegslegs armsarms.

I can float, tread water, even, dare I say it, swim. But only in the shallow end.

"All you have to do is swim from here to there. It's only one lap."

Yeah, ok, only.

"How about we do this next time?"

But then she reminds me that I only have four lessons left.

"Can we compromise?"

I'm not even sure what a compromise looks like, but she says we can practice for a little bit in the shallow end until I'm ready. If I ever get ready.

So we practice a back stroke and I even attempt a breast stroke.

"We can try diving tomorrow if you want."

But we can't. I know we can't because I have a lot more to learn before I'm ready to swim in the ocean. I haven't even swam for five minutes straight.

"No, I'm ready."

"We only have ten minutes left, we can save it for next lesson."

"No, we can't."

"You can schedule more lessons if you need to. But you've been doing excellent, Jamie! You can swim!"

"I can't schedule more lessons, I'm not ready, and I can't swim."

"You just need to be confident!"

"No, it's not that, his birthday is in one week and I have to find him. He can't spend his birthday alone."

"Who?"

"Bas. My brother."

"Why is he going to spend his birthday alone?"

"Because I don't know where he is . . ."

I was working on my thesis when Bas told me that he was going surfing. I don't even think they let you surf when the sun starts going down. But surfing at 7PM doesn't seem strange when you're only half listening.

We were all home for family dinner, but I was drowning in research.

"I love you."

We were close, for sure, but love was always implied, rarely spoken. That should have been my first clue.

"You too."

I regret saying that. The first, but not the biggest regret of that day.

"Where's Sébastien?"

It was only when Mom came home a little later that I thought it was a little weird that he was going to the beach so late. But only a little.

At 8PM, Dad asked me if Bas was going to be home for games.

"Ask him."

My parents knew how to use cellphones, but they always relied on us.

"I did. He hasn't been responding."

Which, I told Dad, wasn't unusual behavior for Bas.

"You know him when he's swimming. He always leaves his bag in the car."

My parents accepted this answer, and that was that. For a while at least.

"At least he wasn't lying to us." That's what I thought when we found his phone in his car by the beach. He had been gone a long time by then.

The port police had actually found his shirt. But not him.

They wanted to call it an accidental drowning, but that would literally be impossible. Bas was an Olympic-grade swimmer. If anyone knew what they were doing in water, it was him.

Mom wanted to have a funeral for him anyway.

The way your stomach feels on a roller coaster is how our relationship feels now. Uneasy, unsure, waiting for something to drop.

I wanted the search to keep going, but after they found his shirt, the port police were out. The fact that they even gave a damn for a second seemed like a blessing. There was one Black guy on the force, Jim. Maybe he felt something.

He said that they couldn't stop us from searching ourselves. But I didn't know how to swim.

So here I am. And I know Bas is still out there. I just have to learn to swim to find him.

Molly has been quiet up until now, but she asks a question I've been dreading:

"How long ago was that?"

I know that the answer to this question makes me look crazy.

". . . Four months ago . . ."

The clock on the wall makes a big TICK. Our lesson is over.

Scene Eight

The Y pool again.

Jamie   I'm thirty years old and I ALMOST know how to swim. My car mantra is evolving. Molly wants to teach me to dive. I'm not sure. I don't even need to learn how to dive to find Bas.

"Come on! You got this!"

I wish I had as much confidence in myself as she does in me.

"Maybe later."

"No, you're ready. You trust me, right?"

"Of course."

"Then you got this! And you won't be doing it alone. We'll just practice jumping first. I'll hold your hand and we'll both jump in at the same time."

"Promise?"

"Promise."

I feel a little spark of electricity when she grabs my hand. Her hand should be wet, but it isn't at all. She smiles.

"You got this."

And I smile back.

"I got this."

"Three—"

"Ok, wait—"

"Two—"

"Maybe we should—"

"One!"

My legs jump without my brain telling them to, but I did it!! But, where's Molly?

I panic. Three previous swim lessons mean nothing in this moment. I'm thrashing and flailing. All the while, the pool is pulling me

D

E

E

P

E

R

My head flops forwards before my whole world turns blue. Then there's a splash and an arm under my shoulders. The next thing I feel is the wet concrete under my skin. Then I'm throwing up water. And Molly is just there. Eyes so wide.

"Are you ok?!"

"No I'm not ok! You were supposed to jump with me!"

"You were supposed to swim!"

"That's a great apology."

"No, Jamie, I am so so so sorry. I do this with all of my kids and they always swim."

"I'm not one of your kids."

"Wait!"

But I'm as quick on land as she is in water.

"Fuck this shit" is my new car mantra.

Scene Nine

Somewhere. Floating.

Jamie   I don't show up for the next session. Or the next one. Or the next one.

I ignore email after email after email.

One subject line reads: "Is everything ok?"

Another: "I'm sorry."

And I swear the last one says, "I miss you," but that's probably wishful thinking.

The one that says "Please" breaks something in me.

I take my email off my phone.

Scene Ten

At a holy place.

Jamie $50 and twenty minutes later and I'm at Babalawo's. I think we're both pretending.

"So what do you do when you're cursed by Mami Wata?"

I almost don't believe the words I'm saying as they come out of my mouth.

"You must make a sacrifice."

Well, that sounds expensive.

"And you're in luck, because I have one Mami Wata sacrifice box left."

Of course he does! I scoff, a bit louder than I'd hoped.

"You don't believe in Mami Wata do you?"

"She just seems a little mean don't you think?"

Babalawo smiles. He tells me that Mami Wata is a protector.

"I don't know if I'd call what she did to the fisherman's son 'protecting'."

"We don't know what his fate would have been if he stayed on land. She still visits the seas of the Caribbean every night. To watch over the descendants of her people who were taken into slavery. Many of them prayed to her as they were being taken. And many of them still do."

Which doesn't convince me. I'm starting to feel like I shouldn't have come here in the first place.

So I thank him, get up, and just as I'm leaving—

"You still have fifteen minutes."

"I think I got what I needed."

"You need to forgive yourself."

"For what?"

"For waiting."

". . ."

"You didn't know."

I can't tell if he really knows or is just fishing, but I bite.

"So what do I do?"

He gives me a shell, apparently Mami Wata's favorite kind, blessed by one of her most devoted followers. It's from Babalawo's sacrifice box, but he gives it to me for free. And we both ignore the $3.99 sticker on the back of it.

He asks me if I want to ask him anything, and I don't, I really don't, but the words just spill out.

"Will I ever learn how to swim?"

He laughs, but it's a comforting laugh. A big dad laugh. That comes from a place where the heart and stomach meet.

"Of course! But only if you forgive your mother. She's always tried to protect you both. There's a reason she never took you to Haiti."

How does he know about Haiti?! This guy is good.

"Maybe."

"And you have to know that you had nothing to do with your brother's disappearance. We cannot control the actions of others, only our own."

I want to give him something, something that says thank you like how I really mean it, but I just spent $52.50 for fewer than twenty minutes. I opt for a hug instead. Which is weird because I don't hug.

Grieving is weird and expensive.

Scene Eleven

The same day. The beach at night. It all feels a little bit eerie.

Jamie   I haven't eaten since this morning, but I feel energized. Hunger makes you more buoyant, right? Or something. Maybe it's actually carbonation. I down a bottle of mystery soda and wonder if it's actually flat. I was going to go home, but I was just like, why? What use are lessons if I don't actually apply them? And what better time than now, right? Or the present? "In the now"? I chug more soda. It's definitely flat. Molly might be a bad person, but she was a good teacher. I already know how to swim, so why wait?

My phone rings, but I ignore it. Another missed call from Mom.

It's Bas's birthday in a couple hours.

My phone rings again. This time it's Dad. I remember when we were blowing up Bas's phone when he went to the beach. Each missed call added to our anxiety. So I answer.

"Where are you?!"

"Hi to you too, Dad."

"Your mom has been trying to reach you for hours."

"I'm busy."

"Doing what?"

"I'm just busy, Dad, let me call you back."

"So busy that you can't even text Mom back?"

"I'm at the beach."

Silence.

"Come home."

"I can't come home."

I hear Dad tell Mom that I'm at the beach.

"Whatever you're about to do, don't do it."

"I'm going to get Bas."

"Jamie."

"I'm hanging up, Dad."

"It wasn't your fault!"

"What?"

Then he tells me that even though I lied about where Bas was, that it wasn't my fault we waited a day to search for him. I told my parents that Bas told me that he was meeting up with some friends, and was staying with them that night. It's just that I had my deadline. My whole life felt like it was falling apart. I was turning thirty, going through a break-up, finishing my master's . . . And my thesis felt like the only thing that mattered at the time. A shot at finding my purpose. A shitty shot at a shitty purpose.

"If I hadn't said that Bas was probably with friends that night, we would have found him."

"Don't blame yourself. It was our fault. Mom and I knew he was struggling."

I didn't know about the depression. The missed therapy appointments. Any of it. Why hadn't they told me?!

"Because you were struggling too. We figured you had enough on your plate."

Then Mom grabs the phone.

"You know why I never took you and your brother to Haiti? Because there's something in the water. Some people call it history, others Lasirèn. But no one makes it out unchanged. She called out to one of my cousins when I was younger. I didn't want to see her take you too."

"I'm going to find him."

"Jamie, please jus—"

I've never hung up on my mom before, but there's always time for firsts. Like my first swim in the ocean.

The water is surprisingly calm. The sun dips behind the horizon, but I'm not afraid. I walk until the ground disappears and then I'm swimming. I'm actually swimming!

"Bas! Can you see me? I'm swimming!"

The shell bounces against my wrist as I swim. I made a bracelet out of the shell that Babalawo gave me. I don't believe in magic, but I do believe in sentiment.

"I'm coming!"

It's not long before my legs are burning. I also didn't anticipate what it would be like swimming with waves. Even the little ones slap a bit too hard. But I just keep legslegslegslegs armsarms, legslegslegslegs armsarms. And that seems to carry me through a couple more minutes.

When I can't swim anymore, I float on my back. The stars start to poke their way through the sky. And then it starts to lightly rain. But it's surprisingly more refreshing than uncomfortable.

I drift until it feels right. Until I start feeling that feeling when I was in the pool. That feeling worth chasing. The feeling I think Bas was chasing. And I let the ocean take me.

I'm
     s
        i
           n
             k
               i
                 n
                    g.

I'm watching my world blur like this isn't my favorite place to be. It's peaceful in a depressing sort of way.

Bubbles pass by me like memories. No, like actual memories.

I see me and Bas as kids. I see my first pool party. I see the freediving competition in Haiti.

I see parties and vacations and birthdays. Birthdays!

"Bas, it's your birth—"

I don't finish my sentence because I see something in the water. It's him. He's really there.

Brown skin, dark eyes, coarse hair. My little brother Sébastien.

"I knew you'd come."

His lips don't move. But it's like I'm hearing his voice in my head. It sounds like speaking into a shell.

I want to say so much, but all I end up saying is:

"I love you."

"I love you too."

"Mom and Dad aren't going to believe this. We've missed you so much. I can't believe I found you!"

"You learned how to swim."

"It was awful. But it doesn't matter. All that matters is that I found you and you're coming back with me."

I grab his hand, but his grip disappears in my fingers.

"I can't come with you."

"What?"

"I have to stay."

"Bas, you can't sta—"

"It wasn't your fault. Not even a little bit. Hug Mom and Dad for me. Tell them I love them too."

It's not supposed to go like this. I'm supposed to find Bas, take him home, and everything would go back to normal.

"You can't stay! You left us! You left me! You'd rather stay here than be with me? Huh? If that's true then don't say shit like you love me, you're killing me. Is that what you want?"

"You wouldn't understand, Jamie."

"I would if you tell me!"

A big wave rolls over us. Thunder roars above. Bas looks behind him. Is something coming?

But I don't have time to think about it because he pushes me backwards.

"Wait!"

My bracelet gets caught on a rock and I start feeling like I'm drowning. I'm tugging and tugging, but nothing's happening.

"Wait!"

I think I hear thunder above me, or is that laughter?

I'm going on two minutes without air.

Bas has disappeared.

My bracelet snaps in my hands.

"Wait!"

I see something solid in front of me and swim to it with all my strength.

Legslegslegslegs armsarms, legslegslegslegs armsarms!

Almost there!

Almost!

There!

I grab onto it, and then,

something starts pulling me from a
                                          b

                                              o

                                                 v

                                                     e.

Scene Twelve

Somewhere above.

Jamie   My brain is only working in single words.

Man. Boat. Chest.

The man. A boat. My chest.

There's a man. I'm on a boat. My chest hurts.

"You're ok. You're ok."

I look at my wrist. My bracelet is gone.

And then I pass out.

Scene Thirteen

Back at the beach. Sometime later.

Jamie   My parents called the port police as soon as I hung up on Dad. But they said that it was too dark, that they'd have to wait until morning. Someone did go out looking for me though.

Jim. The Black port police officer who helped us look for Bas.

Gotta stick together and shit I guess.

We're on the beach now eating crab sandwiches. I asked him if I could take him out for lunch or dinner to thank him. Or give him my first born or something. He opted for lunch. Good choice.

There's this crab shack on the beach. The banner that reads "famous" is fading. But Jim says I'll love it. And he's not wrong.

"It's tradition. I used to do this with my daughter before she got too old and too cool for me."

"Don't worry, you'll be cool again one day."

Jim laughs. I'm guessing he's old enough to be my dad, but with Black people, you can never tell.

"I have something for you."

"Oh no, you already saved my lif—"

It's my bracelet!

"You had it in your hands when I found you. I figured it meant something."

"Thank you."

"What were you doing out there anyway?"

"I was looking for my brother."

"Did you find him?"

"I did."

"And?"

"I just don't understand it, he didn't want to come home."

"There are some things we'll never understand. Some people call it one of life's wonders, I call it a pile of shit. Excuse my language. But what I do understand is that your brother loves you. I should have never found you that night in the storm. But something led me right to you. Maybe it isn't that he didn't want to be with you, but that he didn't want you to be with him."

And we just sit with that for a moment.

Then, a little sea crab scurries in front of us. Jim throws him a piece of his sandwich.

"Jim!"

"What?"

"That's cannibalism!"

"Oh right."

Jim swats the piece of sandwich away. A seagull snaps it up right on cue.

"Aw look. The little guy's shell is broken. He's probably looking for a new home."

I take my broken bracelet, pop off the shell, and place it in front of the little crab.

He grabs onto it, examines it, shimmies out of his old one, and slides into his new home.

"You think you'll ever go swimming again?"